WITHDRAWN
No longer the property of the
Boston Public Library.
Sale of this material benefits the Library.

KING PHILIP

Indian Leader

Colonial Profiles Series

Dennis Brindell Fradin

Illustrations by Tom Dunnington
Picture Research: Judith B. Fradin

ENSLOW PUBLISHERS, INC.
Bloy St. & Ramsey Ave.　　P.O. Box 38
Box 777　　　　　　　　　　　　Aldershot
Hillside, NJ 07205　　　　Hants GU12 6BP
U.S.A.　　　　　　　　　　　　　　U.K.

Copyright © 1990 by Enslow Publishers, Inc.

All rights reserved.

No part of this book may be reproduced without the written permission of the publisher.

Library of Congress Cataloging-in-Publication Data

Fradin, Dennis B.
   King Philip: Indian leader/ by Dennis Brindell Fradin.
     p. cm.—(Colonial profiles)
   Includes index.
   Summary: Recounts the story of the Wampanoag Indian leader who led an uprising against the New England colonists in the seventeenth century.
   ISBN 0-89490-231-8
   1. Philip, Sachem of the Wampanoags, d. 1676—Juvenile literature. 2. King Philip's War, 1675-1676—Juvenile literature. 3. Wampanoag Indians—Biography—Juvenile literature. 4. Indians of North America—Biography—Juvenile literature. [1. Philip, Sachem of the Wampanoags, d. 1676. 2. Wampanoag Indians—Biography. 3. Indians of North America—Biography. 4. King Philip's War. 1675-1676.]
I. Title. II. Series: Fradin, Dennis B. Colonial profiles.
E99.W2P484   1990
973.2'4—dc19   88-31344
                                     CIP
                                     AC

Printed in the United States of America

10 9 8 7 6 5 4 3 2 1

Illustration Credits:
Tom Dunnington (illustrator), pp. 7, 19, 21, 25, 31, 33, 34-35; Historical Pictures Service, Chicago, pp. 13, 27, 28, 36, 43; Library of Congress, pp. 4, 8, 10, 12, 15, 16, 17, 22, 24, 38, 39, 41.

Cover Illustration by Tom Dunnington.

Contents

Introduction	5
The Indians of New England	7
The Pilgrims Come to Massachusetts	10
Massasoit Meets the Pilgrims	14
Massasoit's Son, Metacomet (Philip)	18
What Happened to Philip's Brother, Alexander	23
Philip Plans a War	26
King Philip's War	30
The Death of King Philip	40
Important Dates	44
Glossary	45
Index	47

King Philip (Metacomet)

Introduction

In the early 1600s, English people began to colonize North America. The North American Indians usually helped the early colonists. They gave them land. They taught them to plant corn. When the colonists were hungry, the Indians often shared their food with them.

But as more colonists arrived, they wanted more land. They sometimes cheated the Indians to get it. Fearing that they would one day have no more land, the Indians began to fight.

One of the first chiefs to wage war against the colonists was named Metacomet. He is better known by his English name—King Philip. In 1675-76 Philip led his Wampanoags of Massachusetts and Rhode Island plus several other tribes against the colonists.

The colonists not only won King Philip's War. They also wrote the history books once Philip was dead. Philip was called a "monster" and a "wild beast" in those books. But he was no monster. Like later chiefs, Philip believed that he had to fight to keep some of his people's land.

The Indians of New England

For hundreds of years, the Indians had America to themselves. Many tribes lived in what is now the New England region in the northeastern United States. A typical Indian village had several hundred people living in it.

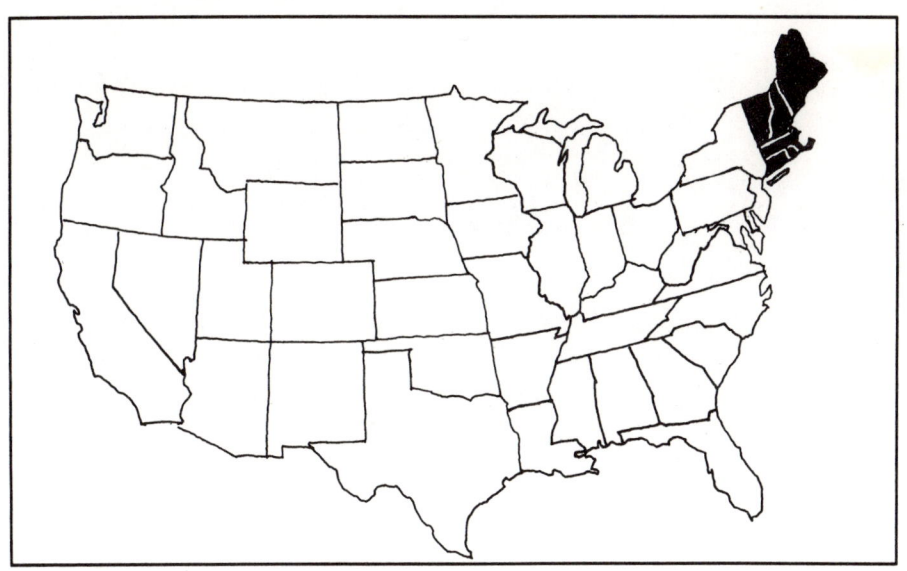

The New England region (in black) is in the northeastern corner of the United States.

The Indians lived in homes made of thin tree trunks and bark. They grew corn and beans. They hunted deer and bears in the forests. They fished in the region's sparkling lakes and streams.

Plants and animals provided the Indians with more than food. Animal skins were turned into clothes and blankets. Bones became needles and fishing hooks. Cornhusks were made into baskets and dolls. The Indians also made deerskin balls that they used to play a game like soccer.

An Indian village in the eastern United States

In two big ways, the Indians differed from the Europeans across the Atlantic Ocean. The Europeans worshiped one God. The Indians thought there were many gods. To the Indians, even animals had spirits. They put unused parts of animals they had killed back in the animals' homes. They thought this made the animals' spirits happy.

The Indians also did not fight like the Europeans. The Europeans frowned on sneak attacks. They thought it was wrong to harm prisoners. The Indians were very loving to their friends and families. But once war broke out, *nothing* was too bad for their foes. They attacked villages at dawn. They tortured prisoners. Later, when Europeans arrived, the Indians did not understand their rules of war. Was not the purpose of war to destroy one's enemies?

The Pilgrims Come to Massachusetts

English explorers and traders began coming to New England in the early 1600s. Some were friendly to the Indians. Others were cruel. Several kidnapped Indians and took them to

Indians watching the arrival of an English ship

Europe. There the Indians were sold as slaves or shown like circus freaks. The Indians grew distrustful when they saw ships coming.

In 1620 New England's first permanent English settlers arrived. Called the Pilgrims, they had left England because they had no religious freedom there. Their ship, the *Mayflower,* reached what is now Massachusetts in November.

Explorers left the *Mayflower* and searched for a good place to build a colony. One party was attacked by Indians. An English trader had kidnapped some of these Indians' men a few years before. The Pilgrim explorers had fewer men, but they had guns. They drove off the Indians, who had only bows and arrows.

In late December 1620 the Pilgrims chose a spot in what is now southeastern Massachusetts. They began building a town called Plymouth there. Plymouth was the second permanent English town in America. The first was Jamestown, Virginia, which had been founded in 1607.

As the Pilgrims built Plymouth, the Indians watched from a distance. Seeing that the English meant them no harm, the Indians came closer. By spring 1621, some of them were very near Plymouth.

The Pilgrims were afraid that the Indians would attack. Of the 102 colonists who had arrived in late 1620, just 50 were alive by spring 1621. In March the men of Plymouth were talking over the Indian problem. Suddenly a tall Indian walked into their midst. "Welcome, Englishmen!" he said to the shocked men.

The Indian, Samoset, had learned English from fishermen near his home in Maine. Samoset told the Pilgrims about the Indians of Massachusetts. Then he shared their duck dinner with them. That night Samoset slept in a Pilgrim family's house.

Samoset soon brought his friend Squanto to Plymouth. Squanto knew English well because he

The building of Plymouth

had been to England. He had been kidnapped by an English sea captain. The captain had tried to sell Squanto as a slave in Europe. But Squanto had escaped. He had returned home by serving as guide to another English sea captain.

During Squanto's absence all his people had died of a disease they had caught from European explorers. Squanto was his tribe's last living member. He was glad to have the Pilgrims for company. That spring he taught the Pilgrims to plant corn. He showed them the best fishing spots. Squanto played a big part in helping the little colony survive.

Samoset entering Plymouth

Massasoit Meets the Pilgrims

The region's leading Indian learned of Squanto's and Samoset's visits to Plymouth. His name was Massasoit, meaning "Great Chief." He led the Wampanoags of present-day eastern Rhode Island and southeastern Massachusetts.

Massasoit loved peace. He was highly intelligent. He wanted the Pilgrims to know that they were welcome. He hoped to obtain tools and guns from them. And he wanted their help if his Wampanoags were attacked by their old enemies, Rhode Island's Narragansetts.

With about 60 warriors, Massasoit left his home at Mount Hope, in present-day Bristol, Rhode Island. They walked to the outskirts of Plymouth. Massasoit camped on a hill while Squanto went back and forth between him and the Pilgrims. Finally, Squanto arranged for Massasoit to meet Governor John Carver in Plymouth.

Massasoit painted his face red. He put on his squirrel coat. Then he entered Plymouth and sat down with Governor Carver in March 1621. Squanto translated as the two leaders made a peace treaty. They vowed that their people would be friends. And they promised to help each other in case a third group attacked.

Other Indians besides Massasoit, Squanto, and Samoset made friends with the English. In fall 1621 the Pilgrims held a feast. During it they thanked God for helping them through their first year in America. Massasoit and about 90 other Indians (probably including Squanto) came to this

Massasoit and his warriors entering Plymouth

The meeting of Chief Massasoit and Governor John Carver

Thanksgiving. This was the start of the Thanksgiving now held every November in the United States.

Massasoit became very friendly with the Plymouth official Edward Winslow. In 1623 Massasoit sent word to Plymouth that he was dying. Edward Winslow went to the great chief and nursed him back to health. There were many other acts of friendship between the Indians and the early colonists.

Edward Winslow, who became friendly with Massasoit

Massasoit's Son, Metacomet (Philip)

Massasoit had five known children. Two were girls—Amie and a second whose name is unknown. He had three sons—Wamsutta, Metacomet, and Suconewhew.

Metacomet, the middle son, was born around 1639. His place of birth is not known, but it may have been his father's village at Mount Hope in Rhode Island. Nothing is known of Metacomet's early years, either. Perhaps as a child he played with a little bow and arrow. Later, he probably took part in foot races and archery contests. In his teens he may have spent time alone in the woods with just his bow and arrow and a knife. This was to show that he could survive on his own.

One of the first known events in Metacomet's life took place when he was about 17. In 1656 Massasoit brought Wamsutta and Metacomet to Plymouth. He asked that they be given English

Philip hunting by himself

names. The English named Wamsutta Alexander. Metacomet they called Philip—the name he is usually known by today.

Philip and his brothers thought their father should not have befriended the English. They saw that the English helped the Indians in some ways. English tools made their work easier. Guns bought from the English were better weapons than bows and arrows. But Philip and his brothers also saw the Indians suffering because of the colonists.

The main problem was that the newcomers kept taking land. The Plymouth Colony had soon grown beyond the town of Plymouth. Also in 1628, English settlers had begun another colony north of the Plymouth Colony. This one was called the Massachusetts Bay Colony. It included Boston and fanned out across much of Massachusetts not claimed by the Plymouth Colony.

The colonists had ways to cheat the Indians in land deals. The deals were written in English. Sometimes the Indians did not know how much land they were selling. If the Indians refused to sell, the colonists might get them drunk to change their minds.

The colonists also tried to make the Indians give up their religion. They wanted them to become Christians. The English called the ones who became Christians Praying Indians. Starting in 1651 they sent them to live in special "Praying Towns." Even the non-Christian Indians were told to obey the colonists' rules. In Massachusetts Bay, Indians who cursed with God's name were punished. In the Plymouth Colony, Indians could not work, fish, or hunt on Sundays.

The Indians said that the English God was not their god. They said that Sunday was not their

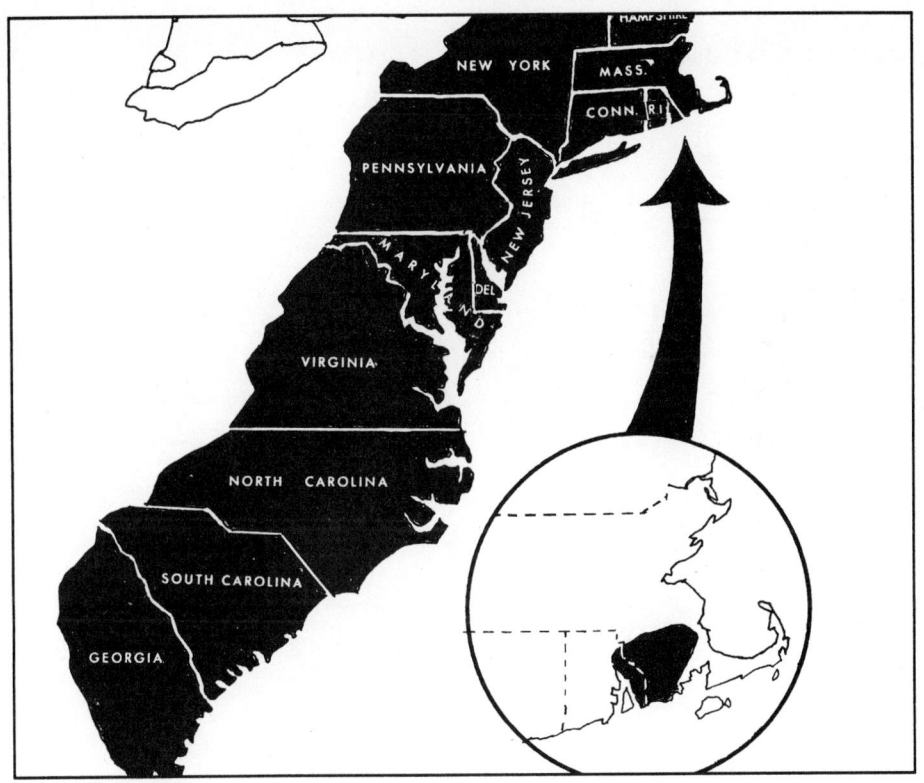

Philip and his Wampanoags lived in eastern Rhode Island and southeastern Massachusetts. That region is shown as the shaded area of the map in the circle.

holy day. But the English tried to make the Indians do things their way anyway. Also, quarrels between Indians and colonists were usually settled in English courts.

Massasoit was upset. But he felt he could not stop the English from changing his people's way of life. The English were too strong. There were too many of them. By 1660, 35,000 colonists lived in New England. The Indians had half that number, and they were not as well armed. Not only that, but Massasoit had vowed to keep peace. He kept his word for 40 years, all the way until he died in 1661 at about the age of 80.

The Indians had not realized that more and more colonists would come and take more and more of their land.

What Happened to Philip's Brother, Alexander

When Massasoit died, his oldest son, Alexander, became Wampanoag chief. Soon the Plymouth colonists learned that Alexander was plotting against them. Alexander was ordered to come prove his loyalty. He refused.

The English sent soldiers to arrest Alexander in summer 1662. They were led by Major Josiah Winslow, son of Massasoit's friend Edward Winslow. The soldiers found Alexander at his hunting lodge a few miles from Plymouth. He and his fellow hunters were feasting. The soldiers seized the guns that were stacked outside. Then they burst into the lodge.

Major Winslow told Alexander that he must go stand trial for plotting against the English. Alexander would not budge. Winslow then pointed a gun at him. "If you refuse, you are a dead man," he said.

Alexander, his wife Weetamoo, and some

friends went with the Englishmen. On the way, Alexander took sick. When he reached the Plymouth Colony, he was asked questions. But he was too ill to stand trial. He was treated by a doctor and then allowed to head home.

By this time Alexander was so sick that his friends had to carry him. When they saw that he was dying, the Indians laid Alexander down beneath a tree. He died, it was said, with his head resting in Weetamoo's lap.

Philip then became Wampanoag chief. He was only about 23 years old when this happened in

The death of Philip's brother, Alexander

1662. King Philip, as the colonists now called him, was enraged by Alexander's death. He believed that Alexander had become ill because the English had made him go with them. He thought Weetamoo's idea that the English doctor had poisoned Alexander might be true. His brother's death was one more thing that Philip held against the colonists.

Philip thinking about all the injustices done to his people

Philip Plans a War

At his home at Mount Hope, Philip brooded. His father had let the English settle on Indian lands. In return the English had taken more and more land. The way things were going, one day the English might have *all* the land. "Little remains of my ancestors' domain," Philip told an English friend. "I am resolved not to see the day when I have no country."

Philip decided to drive the English away. But that was easier said than done. Shortly before Philip's birth, Connecticut's Pequot Indians had fought the English. The Pequots had not been helped by other tribes. In fact, the English had talked several tribes into helping them against the Pequots. As a result, the Pequots had been almost wiped out during the Pequot War of 1636-37.

Philip knew that his people would lose, too, if they fought alone. They needed help from other New England Indians. Then, at the right time,

On June 5, 1637, colonists from Connecticut and Massachusetts burned about 700 Pequot Indians alive in southeastern Connecticut.

King Philip. The "P" below the portrait was the mark he used for signing his name.

they could attack all of New England and drive the colonists away. Getting help from other tribes was not easy. Indians usually disliked siding with warriors of other tribes.

Philip spoke to other tribes. He convinced many warriors to help him. The colonists learned that Philip was plotting something, but they did not know what. They made him come to them several times and swear that he was their friend.

In spring 1671 the colonists made Philip sign a paper. In it he admitted "the Naughtiness of my Heart." At a big meeting in Plymouth a few months later, he was forced to say that the English were his people's rulers. Also in 1671, English officials seized many of his men's guns and gave them to the colonists.

"My father gave them what they asked," Philip reportedly said about the taking of the guns. "They have had townships and whole Indian kingdoms for a few blankets, hoes, and flattering words. But they are not content."

Philip and his men obtained more guns. A few Englishmen sold them some. Dutchmen in New York and Frenchmen in Canada also sold them arms. By early 1675 Philip felt that in a year he and his men would be ready to fight.

King Philip's War

Philip had an aide whose Indian name was Wussausmon. The English called this man John Sassamon. Raised by the English as a Christian, John Sassamon had gone to Harvard College. Later he had returned to his people. Sassamon taught Philip and some of his men to read and write a little English. Sassamon also wrote letters to the English for Philip.

Philip thought that Wussausmon, or John Sassamon, was loyal to him. But near the start of 1675, Sassamon told Plymouth Colony officials about Philip's plot. Sassamon's body was soon found in a frozen pond. Everyone believed that Philip had ordered Sassamon killed for being a traitor. Three of Philip's men were accused of the crime. They were found guilty in an English court. Two of them were hanged on June 8, 1675. The third was later shot.

Philip was a few months away from being

It was thought that Philip had ordered Sassamon killed for being a traitor.

ready for war. But he was afraid that the English would try to arrest him and his men. Philip decided to attack at once. His first target was a town close to Mount Hope—Swansea in the Plymouth Colony.

Years before, a Swansea man had helped Philip's family. Massasoit had told Philip to always protect this man. Philip told his warriors that this man must be spared. On June 24, 1675, the Indians killed about 10 other people at Swansea. This started what was called King Philip's War.

He had given the order, but Philip had not taken part in the Swansea killings. It was said that Philip cried when he learned of the killings. This was very rare, for Indians were proud of being tough in war. Philip may have cried because he knew a lot of blood would flow on both sides.

Philip was the main Indian leader during the war, which was fought mostly in 1675 and 1676. But there were other Indian leaders. The Narragansetts, under Chief Canonchet, helped Philip. Weetamoo, wife of Philip's dead brother, was chief of the small Pocasset tribe. Several hundred of Weetamoo's warriors fought for Philip. So did several hundred men under Awashonks—woman chief of the small Sakonnet tribe. And the Nipmuc tribe was very helpful to Philip's cause.

The Indians attacked about half of New England's 100 or so towns during the war. Present-day Massachusetts was hardest hit. The Indians set towns ablaze by shooting flaming arrows at rooftops. They also rolled flaming wagons against the houses. As the colonists ran from their burning homes, the Indians shot or tomahawked them. Among the towns that were attacked were Lancaster, Springfield, and Brook-

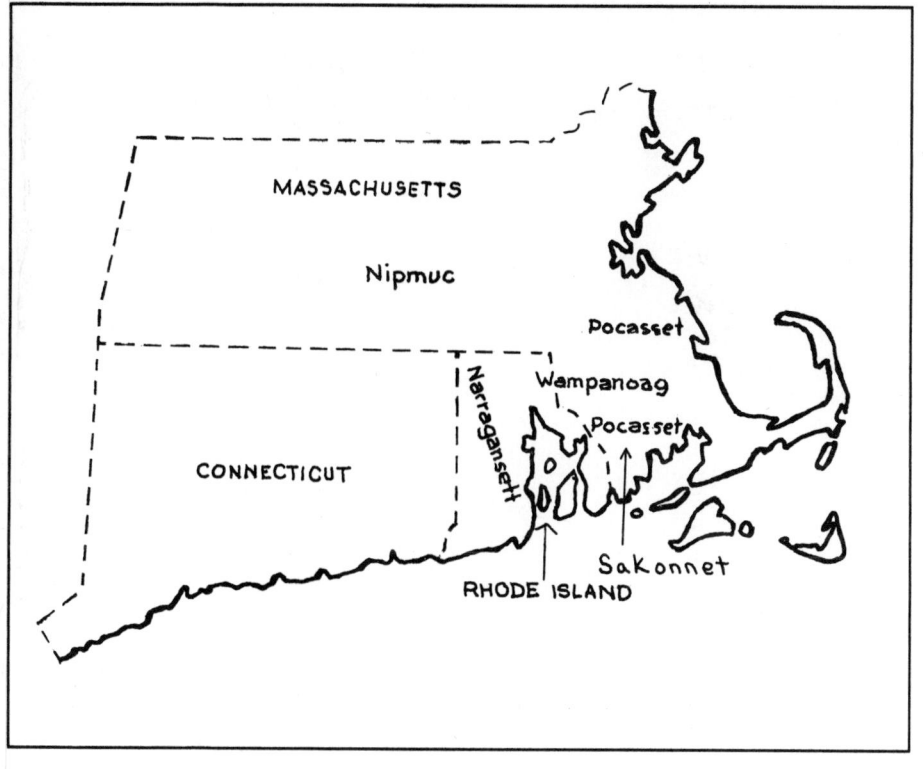

Indian tribes of King Philip's War

field in Massachusetts and Providence in Rhode Island.

Philip was seen riding a black horse when the Indians killed about 20 colonists at Medfield, Massachusetts. He was said to have been at the killing of about 20 soldiers near Northfield, Massachusetts. But he probably planned many other battles without fighting in them. However, Philip may have been at some battles without the colonists knowing it. Philip knew the colonists wanted to kill him more than any other Indian.

He sometimes cut his hair or wore disguises to hide who he was.

Most colonists viewed Philip and his people as evil. Philip was called a "savage and wild beast" and a "hellish monster." His people were called "rabid animals" and "devils." The colonists called themselves "honest, harmless Christians."

But the colonist who knew Philip best during the war did not agree. She was Mary Rowlandson of Lancaster, Massachusetts. In the attack on Lancaster, Mrs. Rowlandson was captured. She was

Philip on his black horse leading an attack

The attack on Brookfield, Massachusetts

held for three months, until the colonists paid to free her.

Mrs. Rowlandson later wrote about the experience. She described Philip as quiet and polite. She also told how she made a shirt and cap for Philip's son. Philip thanked her by giving her money and asking her to dinner.

Philip also warned colonists who had been kind to his people that attacks were coming. At one point he wrote this touching note to Plymouth officials:

> You know and we know your heart great sorrowful with crying for your lost many many hundred men and all your house and all your land and woman, child and cattle as all your thing that you have lost. . . .

Because to them the Indians were "devils," the colonists put aside their rules of war. They imprisoned several thousand "Praying Indians," even though they had not helped Philip. The colonists also tortured some captives. But their cruelest deed came late in 1675 at a Narragansett Indian village in Rhode Island.

These Narragansetts had sheltered many of Philip's Wampanoags. On December 19, 1675, one thousand soldiers from Massachusetts Bay, Connecticut, and Plymouth marched to this village. Some of their Indian friends went with them. The soldiers set the village on fire. Hundreds of men, women, and children were burned to death. Those who tried to escape were shot. About a thousand Indians died at this Great Swamp Fight.

Philip had many close calls during the war. Once he and his men escaped from a swamp where they were trapped by floating across the water on canoes and rafts at night. He may have escaped from the Great Swamp Fight in disguise. Or perhaps he was not there. In any case, the day was coming when Philip would not be able to escape.

The slaughter of the Indians at the Great Swamp Fight probably looked something like this, although the Indians wore clothes.

Philip saw that the tide was turning against him.

The Death of King Philip

Philip and his men won some battles after the Great Swamp Fight. But the tide turned in favor of the colonists in 1676. Many of Philip's friends and relatives were killed or captured. Seeing that they would lose, many of Philip's people left him. Some even switched to the colonists' side.

Then on August 1, 1676, Philip took an awful blow. That day his wife and son were captured by Captain Benjamin Church, of what is now Rhode Island. They were later sold abroad as slaves along with other Indian captives.

After the capture of his wife and son, Philip went home to Mount Hope. He had probably not been there during the war. It was a place where he could easily be trapped. Now Philip no longer seemed to care, and some people thought he even wanted to die. Captain Church learned that Philip was at Mount Hope. He headed there with his soldiers and Indian friends.

On the night of August 11, Philip was sleeping outside at Mount Hope when he awoke from a nightmare. He told a friend that he had dreamed of being captured.

Church and his men approached at dawn of August 12, 1676. Seeing Church's forces, Philip leaped to his feet and ran. A colonist aimed his gun at Philip, but it would not fire. One of the

Benjamin Church

colonists' Indian allies then aimed and fired. Philip fell face down in the mud—dead.

Soon after Philip's death, the war ended in most of New England, although it lasted several more years in Maine and New Hampshire. The war had been terrible for both sides. About a thousand colonists and several thousand Indians had been killed. The Wampanoag and Narragansett tribes had been nearly wiped out.

For many years, New England children were told stories about how the "wild beast," King Philip, had been killed. But Philip had only fought to save his homeland. Wouldn't the colonists have done the same thing had they been in his place?

The death of King Philip

Important Dates

1607 Jamestown (Virginia), England's first permanent town in what is now the United States, is founded.

1620 Pilgrims found Plymouth, England's first settlement in Massachusetts.

1621 In the spring Philip's father, Massasoit, makes a peace treaty with the Pilgrims; that fall he attends the Pilgrims' first Thanksgiving.

1639 Metacomet (later known as King Philip) is born around this year.

1661 Massasoit dies.

1662 Philip's brother, Alexander, dies; Philip becomes Wampanoag chief.

1671 Philip is forced to sign paper admitting his "Naughtiness."

1675 King Philip's War begins in June; Indians are slaughtered at Great Swamp Fight in December.

1676 On August 1, Philip's wife and son are captured and later sold as slaves; Philip is killed at Mount Hope on August 12.

Glossary

allies—friends or helpers, especially in wartime.

ancestors—earlier relatives.

captives—people held against their will.

colonists—people who settle in a land outside their home country.

colony—a settlement built by a country outside its borders.

domain—home region.

naughtiness—badness.

permanent—lasting.

Pilgrims—the people who built Plymouth, England's first settlement in Massachusetts.

Praying Indians—Indians who became Christians in colonial America.

traitor—someone who works against his or her country or people.

translate—to take words and put them in another language.

INDEX

Alexander, 20. *See also* Wamsutta.
    arrest of, 23
    as chief of the Wampanoags, 23
    death of, *24*
Awashonks, 32-33

Brookfield, Massachusetts, attack on, 33-34, *36*

Canonchet, chief of the Narragansetts, 32
Carver, Governor John, 14, 15
    meeting with Chief Massasoit, *16*
    peace treaty with, 15, 22
Church, Captain Benjamin, 40, *41*

Great Swamp Fight, 37-*38*, 40

Indians of New England, 7
    and early colonists, 5, 10-13
    foods of, 8
    games of, 8
    lifestyle of, 8, 9
    map of, *33*
    punishment of, 21
    suffering under the English by, 5, 10-11, 20
    typical village of, *8*
    war practices of, 9

Jamestown, Virginia, 11

Massachusetts, 11, 12, 14, 20, *21*, 33-34
Massachusetts Bay Colony, 20, 21, 27
Massasoit, chief of the Wampanoags, 14
    children of, 18, 20
    death of, 22
    and Edward Winslow, 17
    at first Thanksgiving, 15, 17
    meeting with Governor John Carver, *16*
    peace treaty with, 15, 22
    visit to Plymouth, 14, *15*
Mayflower, 11
Metacomet. *See* Philip, King.
Mount Hope, Rhode Island, 14, 18, 26, 32, 40, 41

Narragansetts of Rhode Island, 14, 32, *33*, 37, *38*, 42
New England
    arrival of Europeans to, 5, *10*, 11, 22
    map of, 7

Nipmuc tribe, *33*

Pequot War, 26, *27*
Philip, King, 5, *21*
    appearance of, *4, 28*
    birth of, 18
    capture of his wife and son, 40
    as chief of the Wampanoags, 24-*25*
    death of, 40-42, *43*
    hunting, *19*
    King Philip's War, 5, 30-*39*
      attack on Swansea, 32
      leading attack during, *34-35*
      plotting of, 26, 29
      towns attacked during, 33-34, 35, *36*
      tribes of, *33*
    "Naughtiness of my Heart" meeting, 29
    renaming of, 18, 20
    signature of, *28*
Pilgrims
    arrival in New England of, *10*, 11
    religious beliefs of, 9, 21
Plymouth Colony, 20, 21, 24, 30
Plymouth, Massachusetts, 11, *12*, 14, 15, 18, 23, 37
Pocasset tribe, 32, *33*
"Praying Indians," 20-21, 37

Rhode Island, 5, 14, 18, *21, 33*, 34, 37
Rowlandson, Mary, 35, 37

Sakonnet tribe, 33
Samoset, 12, *13*, 14, 15
Sassamon, John, 30, *31*
Squanto, 12-13, 14, 15
Suconewhew, 18

Thanksgiving feast, 15, 17

Wampanoag Indians of Rhode Island & Massachusetts, 5, 14, 42
    map of, *21*
Wamsutta, 18
    renaming of, 20
Weetamoo, wife of Alexander, 23, 24, 32
Winslow, Edward, *17*
    nursing Massasoit, 17
Winslow, Major Josiah, 23
Wussausmon. *See* Sassamon, John.